Alfred's Kid's Guitar Course

The Easiest Guitar Method Ever!

Ron Manus • L. C. Harnsberger

Alfred Music
P.O. Box 10003
Van Nuys, CA 91410-0003
alfred.com

ISBN-10: 0-7390-6249-2 (Book & CD)
ISBN-13: 978-0-7390-6249-4 (Book & CD)

Audio recording performed by Jared Meeker.

Cover and interior illustrations by Jeff Shelly.

Contents

Tracks 1 & 2

Tuning Your Guitar

The CD contains all the warm-ups and tunes in Book 3, so you may listen and play along with them. You need to be sure your guitar is in tune every time you start to play, especially when you want to play along with the CD. Listen carefully to the instructions on Track 1, then use Track 2 to get your guitar in tune.

Book 2 Review

Before starting this book, you need to know the following things that were taught in *Alfred's Kid's Guitar Course, Book 2* as well as everything taught in Book 1. If there's anything you don't remember, go back to Book 2 and review it. Once you are comfortable with all these things, get started with Book 3!

Notes

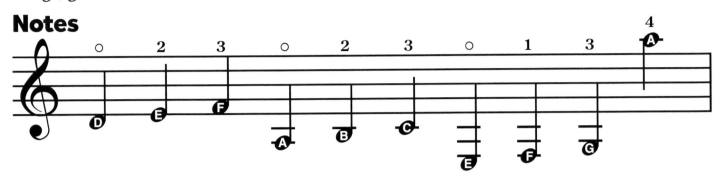

Chords

The four-string
C chord

The four-string
G chord

The four-string
G7 chord

Reading 3- and 4-note chords as notes

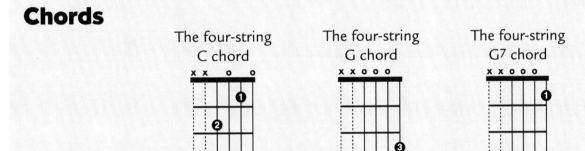

Bass-chord accompaniments

Rhythms

| Half Note Slash | Dotted Half Note | Dotted Half Note Slash | Whole Rest | Tie | Fermata |

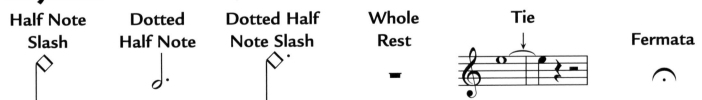

Time Signatures

$\mathbf{C}$ = Common Time = $\frac{4}{4}$

$\frac{3}{4}$ = 3 beats in each measure
A quarter-note gets 1 beat

Tempo signs: Andante, Moderato, Allegro
Dynamics: p, mf, f, ff

Playing two notes at once
Ledger lines
Pickup measures

Introducing B-Flat

Hear this note! Track 3

A flat ♭ lowers a note a *half step* (the distance from one fret to another is called half step). B♭ is played one fret lower than the note B. When a flat note appears in a measure, it is still flat until the end of that measure.

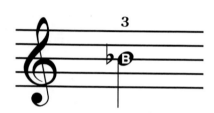

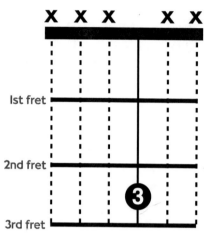

1st fret

2nd fret

3rd fret

B-Flat Bop

Track 4

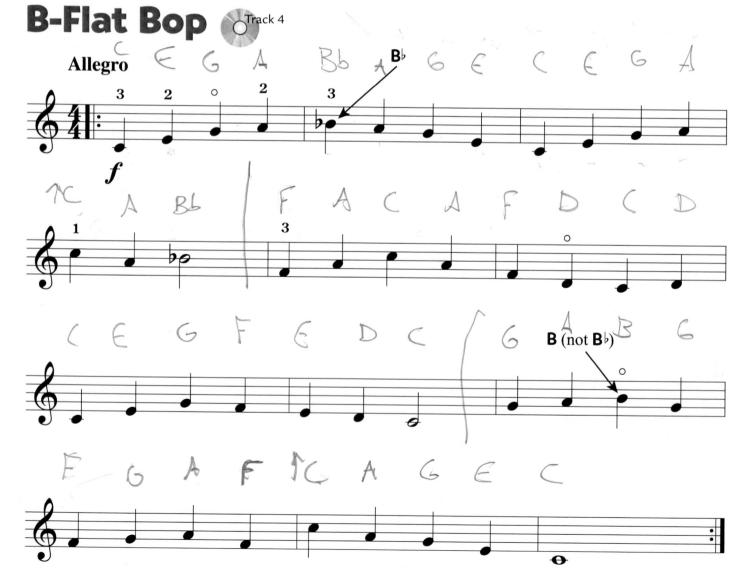

4

Good Night Ladies

Track 5

Moderato

| A | F | C | F | A | F | G | G |

Good night, la - dies Good night, la - dies

mf

| A | F | B♭ | B♭ | B♭ | A | A | G | G | F | **C** |

Good night, la - dies We're going to leave you now____

| A | G | F | G | A | A | A | G | G | G | A | C | C |

Mer - ri - ly we roll a - long Roll a - long, roll a - long.

| A | G | F | G | A | A | A | G | G | A | G | F |

Mer - ri - ly we roll a - long O'er the deep blue sea

5

Key Signatures

The key signature at the beginning of a piece tells you when a note is played as a flat note throughout the piece. In "Ode to Joy (Extended Version)," each B is played as B-flat. The high B and low B are both played B-flat.

Ode to Joy (Extended Version) Track 6

Key Signature: remember to play each B one half step lower.

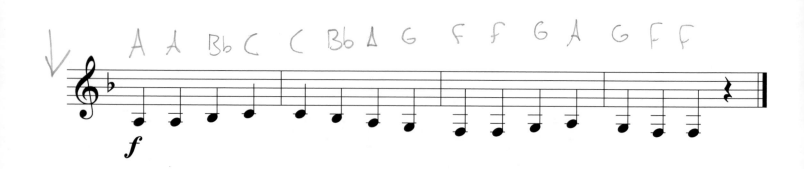

6

Eighth Notes

Eighth notes are black notes with a flag added to the stem: ♪ or ♩.
Two or more eighth notes are written with beams: ♫ or ♫, ♬ or ♬.
Each eighth note receives one half beat.

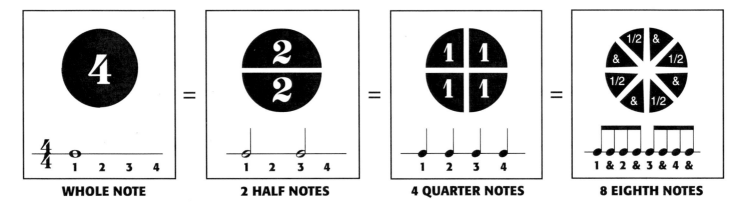

| WHOLE NOTE | 2 HALF NOTES | 4 QUARTER NOTES | 8 EIGHTH NOTES |

Use alternating downstrokes ⊓ and upstrokes ∨ on eighth notes.

Track 7

Count: 1 & 2 & 3 & 4 &   1 & 2 & 3 & 4 &

Before you play eighth notes on your guitar, clap the rhythms
in the picking example above while you count the eighth
notes as "one-and two-and three-and four-and." Make sure
all the notes are even.

Jammin' with Eighth Notes Track 8

Allegro Moderato*

Count: 1   2   3   4   1 & 2 & 3 & 4 & (etc.)

*Allegro moderato means moderately fast.

Clementine

Moderato

In a cav - ern, in a can - yon Ex - ca - vat - ing for a

G⁷

mine   Dwelt a min - er   for - ty - nin - er   And his

C

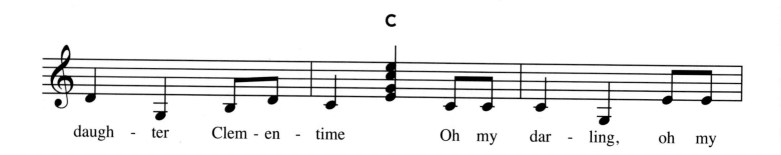

daugh - ter   Clem - en - time   Oh my dar - ling,   oh my

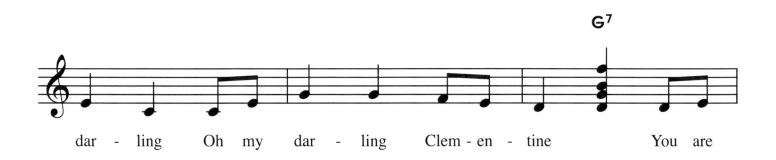

dar - ling Oh my dar - ling Clem - en - tine You are

lost and gone for - ev - er Dread-ful sor - ry, Clem-en - tine

Additional Verses

Verse 2
Light she was and like a fairy,
And her shoes were number nine,
Herring boxes, without topses,
Sandals were for Clementine.

Chorus
Oh my darlin', oh my darlin',
Oh my darlin' Clementine!
You art lost and gone forever
Dreadful sorry, Clementine.

Verse 3
Drove she ducklings to the water
Every morning just at nine,
Hit her foot against a splinter,
Fell into the foaming brine.

Chorus
Oh my darlin', oh my darlin',
Oh my darlin' Clementine!
You art lost and gone forever
Dreadful sorry, Clementine.

Verse 4
Ruby lips above the water,
Blowing bubbles soft and fine,
But, alas, I was no swimmer,
So I lost my Clementine.

Chorus
Oh my darlin', oh my darlin',
Oh my darlin' Clementine!
You art lost and gone forever
Dreadful sorry, Clementine.

Go Tell Aunt Rhody

Track 10

Moderato

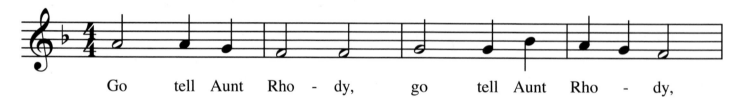

Go   tell   Aunt   Rho - dy,   go   tell   Aunt   Rho - dy,

go   tell   Aunt   Rho - dy   get   up,   get   out   of   bed.

Gray   goose   is   hun - gry,   gray   goose   is   hun - gry,

gray   goose   is   hun - gry   and   is   wait - ing   to   be   fed.

Eighth Note Rock

Track 11

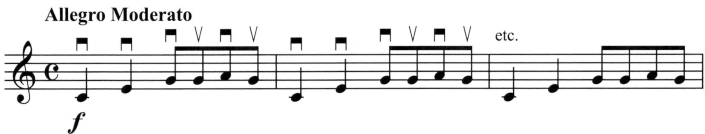

Dotted Quarter Notes

**A DOT INCREASES
THE LENGTH OF A NOTE
BY ONE HALF**

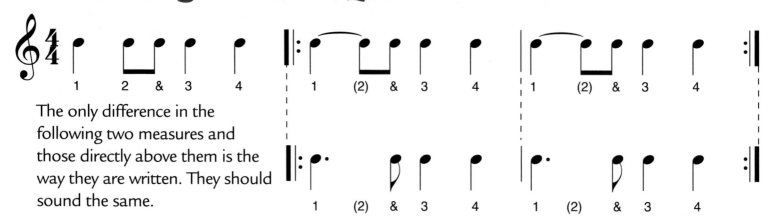

= 3 COUNTS

= 1½ COUNTS

Counting Dotted Quarter Notes

The only difference in the following two measures and those directly above them is the way they are written. They should sound the same.

Cockles and Mussels   Track 12

Moderately

Count: 3   1   2 & 3 &   1 & 2 & 3 &

In Dub - lin's   fair   cit - y,   where   girls   are   so   pret - ty,   I

first   set   my   eyes   on sweet Mol - ly   Ma - lone,   As she

wheeled her wheel - bar - row through streets broad and nar - row, Cry - ing

Cock - les and Mus - sels! a - live, a - live oh!

Chorus

A - live, a - live oh! __ A - live, a - live oh! Cry- ing

Cock - les and Mus - sels! a - live, a - live oh!

Auld Lang Syne

Track 13

Moderato

The Down-and-Up Stroke

Track 14

You can make your accompaniment of waltz songs in $\frac{3}{4}$ like "The Streets of Laredo" more interesting by replacing the second beat of the measure with a downstroke followed by an upstroke. The symbol for downstroke is ⊓; an upstroke uses the symbol V. Together, the down-and-up strokes are two eighth notes that are played in the same time as single quarter note.

Try the following exercise to work just on the new rhythm.

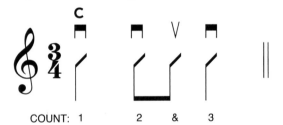

Now practice changing from C to G7.

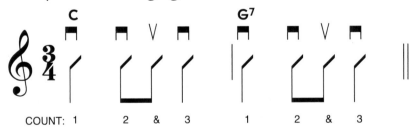

Now practice changing back and forth from C to G7 and back. When you can do it smoothly, go to page 16 and use it to accompany "The Streets of Laredo."

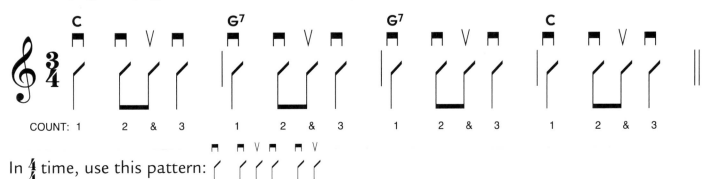

In $\frac{4}{4}$ time, use this pattern:

The Streets of Laredo

Moderately

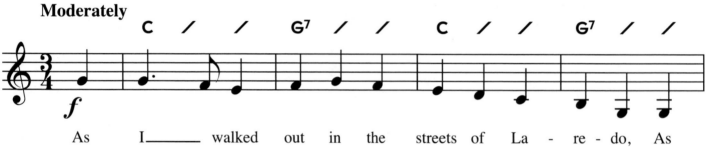

As I_____ walked out in the streets of La - re - do, As

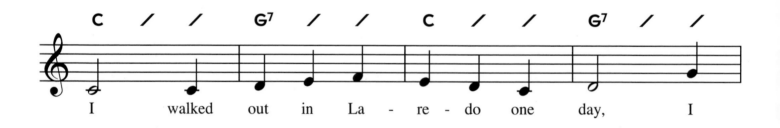

I walked out in La - re - do one day, I

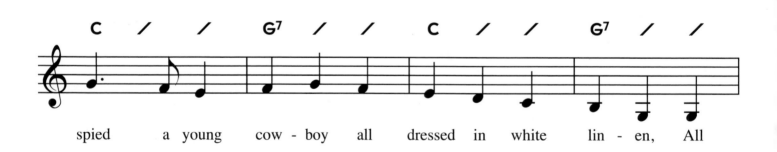

spied a young cow - boy all dressed in white lin - en, All

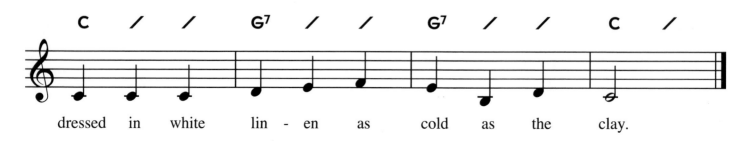

dressed in white lin - en as cold as the clay.

16

Introducing F-Sharp

A sharp ♯ raises a note one half step. F-sharp is played one fret higher than the note F. When a sharp note appears in a measure, it is still sharp until the end of that measure.

Hear this note! Track 16

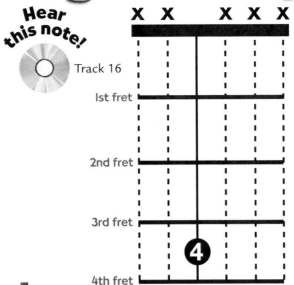

Little Brown Jug

Track 17

Learn both the melody and chords for this song. Use the $\frac{4}{4}$ strumming pattern from the bottom of page 15.

Brightly

My wife and I live all a-lone in a lit - brown hut we call our own; she loves gin, and I love rum, I

tell you what, don't we have fun? Ha, ha, ha, you and me,

lit - tle brown jug, don't I love thee? Ha, ha, ha,

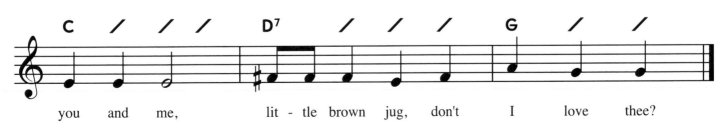

you and me, lit - tle brown jug, don't I love thee?

Introducing
The Four-String D⁷ Chord

This is the same as the three-string D7 chord, but you also strum the open D string. This is your first chord with a sharp note.

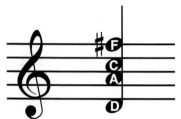

Hear this chord! Track 18

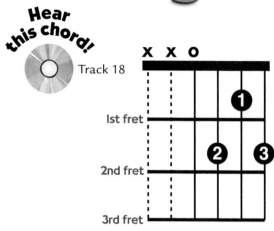

Rockin' the Bach

Track 19

18

Amazing Grace

Learn the solo part and the accompaniment chords for "Amazing Grace" using the ¾ strumming pattern from page 15.

Track 20

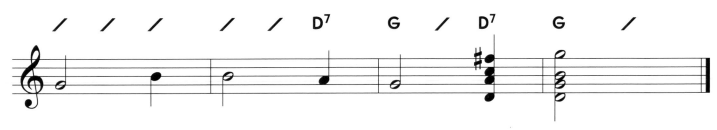

Bass-Chord Accompaniment in ¾

When music is in ¾ time, you can't use the bass-chord accompaniment patterns you already know because they only work in 4/4 time. In ¾, the most common bass-chord accompaniment pattern is bass-chord-chord. First play the bass note alone, then the rest of the chord on beats 2 and 3. Any time you want to play accompaniment chords in ¾ time, use this pattern.

Track 21

Sometimes the chord changes every measure. Practice this example before you play "Cielito Lindo." Don't move on to the song until you can easily play the accompaniment pattern without missing a beat.

Track 22

Cielito Lindo

Play the accompaniment to this famous Mexican folk song and also learn it as a solo.

Track 23

Allegro

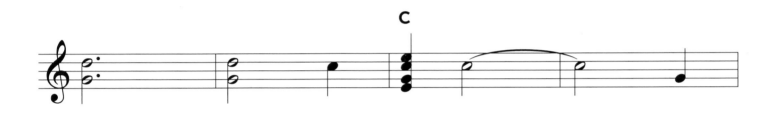

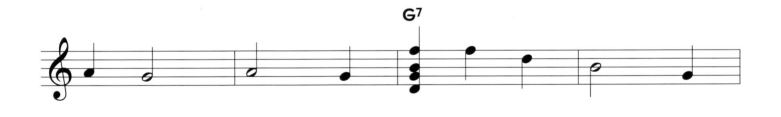

After you master "Cielito Lindo," go back to page 19 and play the chords for "Amazing Grace" using the bass-chord-chord accompaniment pattern.

Sharps ♯, Flats ♭, and Naturals ♮

You already know the notes B-flat and F-sharp, but there are other flat and sharp notes you can play on the guitar.

♯ A sharp raises a note a half step. When you see a sharp in front of any note, it means that note is sharp and it is played one fret higher. The note C-sharp is a half step higher than the note C, which means it is played one fret higher than the note C.

Track 24

♭ A flat lowers a note a half step. When you see a flat in front of any note, it means that note is flat and is played one fret lower. The note A-flat is a half step lower than the note A and is played one fret lower than the note A. This is the same for other flat notes.

Track 25

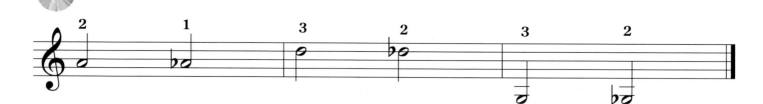

If an open note (open string) is flat, that means to play the 4th fret of the next lower string unless that string is the G string (3rd string), then play the 3rd fret. That means that if you see the note E-flat on the top space of the staff, you finger it on the 4th fret of the second string. But when you see the note B-flat, it is played on the 3rd fret of the 3rd string.

Track 26

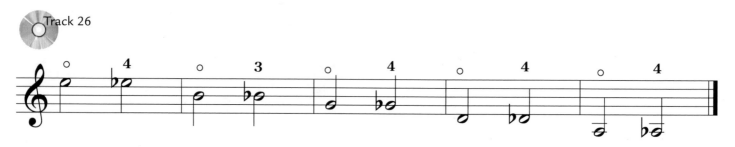

♮ A natural sign cancels a previous sharp or flat. A note that is sharp or flat continues to be flat or sharp in the same measure unless it is cancelled by a natural. Flats and sharps only last until the end of the measure.

Half Steps and Whole Steps

You already know that the distance from one fret to the next fret is called a half step. The distance of two frets is called a WHOLE STEP. In the picture below, you can see half steps on the high E string and whole steps on the low E string.

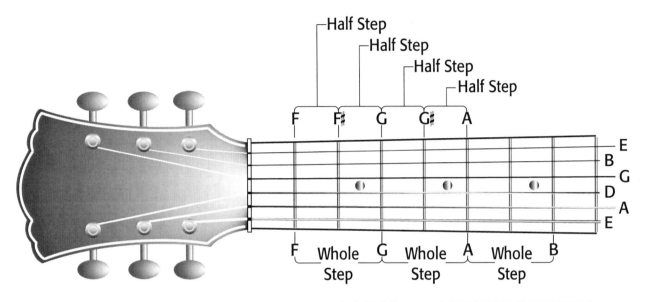

This is what whole and half steps look like on a piano.

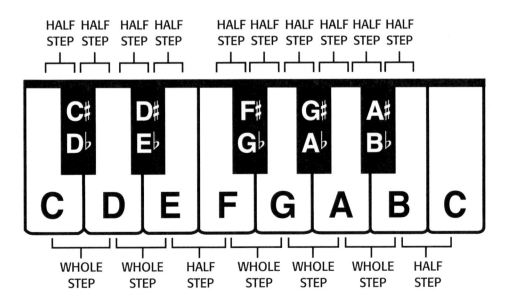

The Chromatic Scale

The *chromatic scale* is made completely out of half steps. Each note is one fret away from the one next to it. A chromatic scale going up is written with sharps. There are two pairs of natural notes that are only a half step away from each other: E to F, and B to C. All the other half steps are sharps or flats.

Chromatic Scale Going Up

Track 27

A chromatic scale going down is written with flats.

Chromatic Scale Going Down

Track 28

24

Chromatic Rock

Track 29

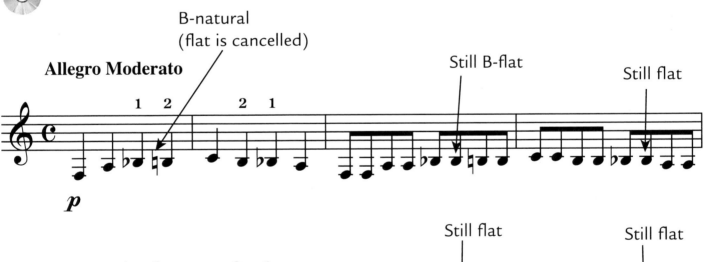

Rockabilly Bass Line

The Four-String D Chord

Use finger 1 and 2 to press the 3rd and 1st strings at the 2nd fret. Use finger 3 to press the 2nd string at the 3rd fret.

Hear this note! Track 31

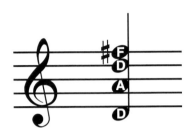

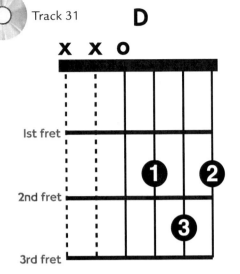

Four-Beat Blues

Track 32

This tune uses sharps, flats, naturals, and the four-string D chord. Play it slowly at first and gradually increase the speed as you become more comfortable playing it.

Moderato

Frankie and Johnny

Track 33

Allegro

28

The Major Scale

A major scale is a group of eight notes in alphabetical order. It is like a puzzle because you need to put whole-step pieces and half-step pieces in the right order to make it sound correct. The pattern of whole steps and half steps is what gives the major scale its distinct sound.

Here is the order of whole and half steps for a major scale:
whole step * whole step * half step * whole step * whole step * whole step * half step

There are two whole steps, followed by one half step, followed by three more whole steps, and then one more half step. In music it looks like this:

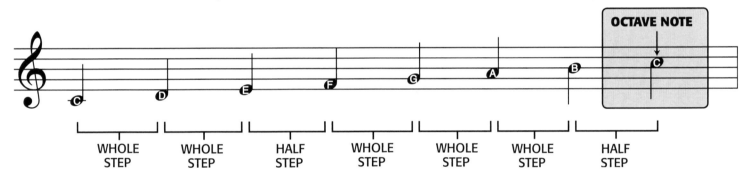

The highest note of the scale has the same letter name as the first note, and is called an *octave*. "Octave" means eight (like an octopus with eight legs), so two notes with the same name but are eight notes apart are called an octave.

Introducing the C Major Scale

When a major scale starts on the note C, it is called a C Major scale. The notes above make up the C Major scale. It is easy to visualize all the whole steps and half steps of a major scale by seeing it on a piano keyboard. Notice there are whole steps between every note except E to F, and B to C.

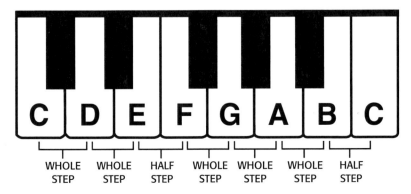

C Major Scale Exercise

Track 34

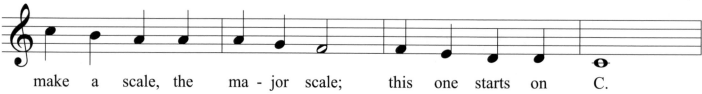

Whole whole half, whole whole whole, and a half step;

make a scale, the ma - jor scale; this one starts on C.

C whole whole half whole whole whole half. Play the scale and try not to laugh!

This Is an Octave

Track 35

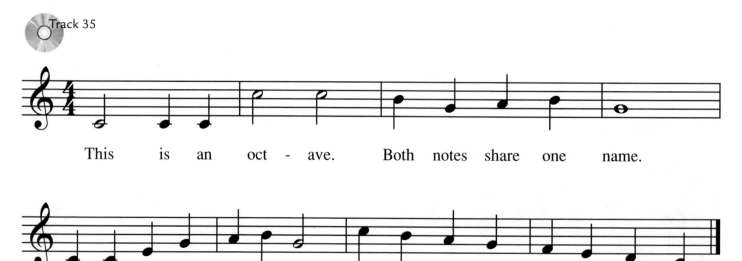

This is an oct - ave. Both notes share one name.

They are just eight notes a - part. One, two, three, four, five, six, seven, eight!

The first three measures of this song use all the notes of the C Major scale in order, from the top of the scale (the high octave) to the bottom (the low octave). This is one of the most popular melodies ever written, and it all comes from the major scale!

Joy to the World

 Track 36

Allegro

31

The G Major Scale

When scales start on notes other than C, you will need a sharp or flat to make the pattern of whole and half steps work out. If you wanted to play "Joy to the World" starting on G, you would have to change one of the notes to make the whole-half formula work. First, play the first four measures without any sharps or flats.

Track 37

Allegro

Now, that doesn't sound quite right. The second note sounds too low! To get the right pattern of whole and half steps for a major scale starting on G, you need to make the F an F-sharp.

Track 38

OCTAVE NOTE

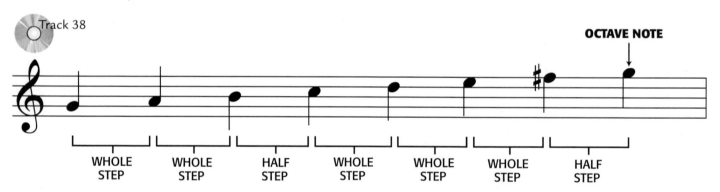

Key Signature

Now if we play "Joy to the World" again with an F-sharp and start on G, it sounds correct. This version of "Joy to the World" below is in the key of G, which has one F-sharp in the key signature. Below, all the F notes are played as F-sharp because the key signature has a sharp on the top F line.

Track 39

Key signature

F-sharp

Allegro

Polly Wolly Doodle

Crescendo and Diminuendo

The sign ◁▷ or the word *crescendo* means to gradually GROW LOUDER.

The sign ▷◁ or the word *diminuendo* means to gradually GROW SOFTER.

Track 40

Moderato

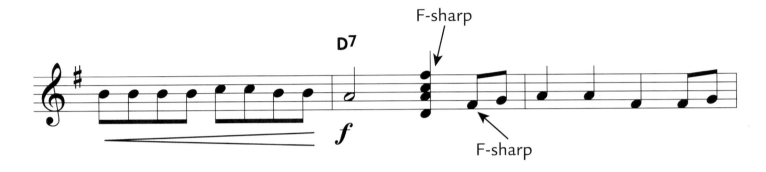

F-sharp

F-sharp

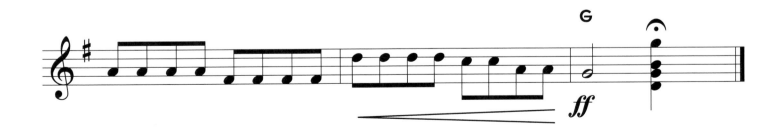

The F Major Scale

If you wanted to play "Joy to the World" starting on F instead of G, you would have to change a different note to make the whole-half formula work.

Here are the first four measures without any sharps or flats.

Track 41

Allegro

This doesn't sound quite right. The fifth note sounds too high! To get the right pattern of whole and half steps for the F Major scale, you need to make the B a B-flat.

Track 42

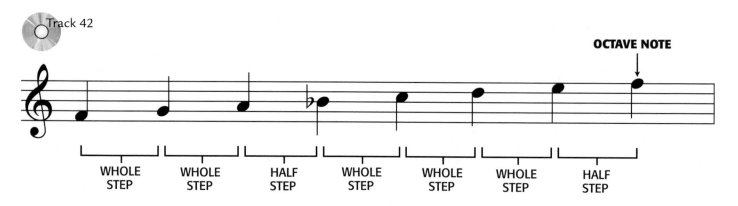

Now if we play "Joy to the World" again with a B-flat and start on F, it sounds correct.

Track 43

Allegro

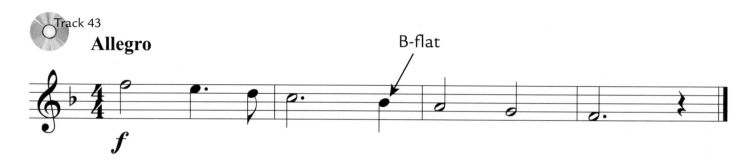

Accidentals

Sometimes songs have sharps and flats in the music that are not in the key signature. Those sharps and flats are called *accidentals*. Accidentals only affect the measure in which they appear. A natural sign can be an accidental if it cancels a sharp or flat in the key signature, but it only affects the note until the end of the measure.

This song is in the key of F. An F-sharp accidental appears twice near the end. Remember they only last until the end of the measure.

Give My Regards to Broadway

Track 44

George M. Cohan

Allegro

B-flat

F-natural

The Man on the Flying Trapeze

This song is in the key of G. Every F is played as F#. There are also some sharp notes that aren't in the key signature that only last for the measure they are in.

Track 45

Introducing Eighth Rests

 This is an EIGHTH REST.
It means REST for the value of an EIGHTH NOTE.

When eighth notes appear by themselves, they look like this: ♪ or ♪.

Single eighth notes are often used with eighth rests: ♪ ⁊ .
Count: "1   &"

Clap and Count Out Loud   Track 46

Count: 1   &   2   &   3   &   4   &

When an eighth rest follows a fingered note, the sound is cut off by releasing the pressure of the finger on the string. When following an open note, the sound is cut off by touching the string with either a left-hand finger or the heel of the right hand.

Eighth Rest Example #1   Track 47

Eighth Rest Example #2   Track 48
Eighth rests may also appear on downbeats. Try to keep an even beat by tapping your foot or silently counting each eighth.

Count: 1   &   2   &   3   &   4   &   (etc.)

Eighth Rest Example #3   Track 49

Count: 1 & 2 & 3 & 4 &   1 & 2 & 3 & 4 &   1 & 2 & 3 & 4 &   1 & 2 & 3 & 4 &

La Bamba

Track 50

Allegro moderato

COUNT: 1   2 &   3   4 & 1 & 2 & etc.

1   2 & 3   4 &

1 & 2 & 3 & 4 &

Three Principal Chords

The three principal chords are the most commonly used chords used in that key. If you number all the notes of a major scale, there are eight total notes. Below are the numbered notes of the G Major scale.

1   2   3   4   5   6   7   8

The three principal chords are the chords based on the 1st, 4th, and 5th notes of the major scale. In the key of G, the three principal chords are G (1), C (4), and D7 (5).

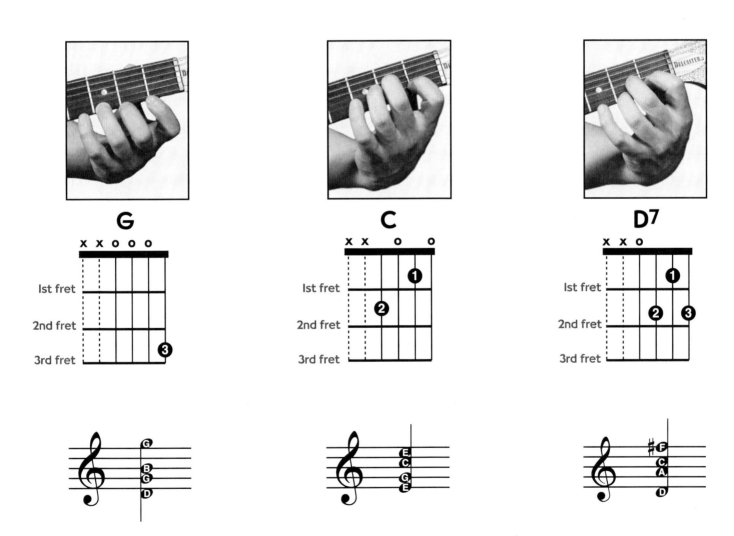

Rockin' with Three Chords in G Track 51

King Louie Rocks

Track 52

Practice this one slowly at first until you can change quickly and smoothly between the chords. *D.S. al Fine* means repeat back to the 𝄋, then play until the word *Fine*, which is the end.

40

Introducing
Five- & Six-String Chords

The Five-String A Chord

Use fingers 1, 2, and 3 to press the 4th, 3rd, and 2nd strings at the 2nd fret. Also, play the 5th and 1st strings open. Three fingers are on the same fret so they might feel squished. Play the chord over and over until all the notes sound good. This is the first chord you are learning that uses five strings.

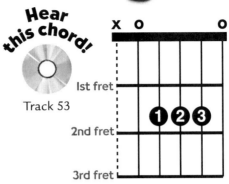

Hear this chord!
Track 53

The Six-String E7 Chord

This chord uses all six strings! Use finger 2 to press the 5th string at the 2nd fret. Use finger 1 to press the 3rd string at the 1st fret.

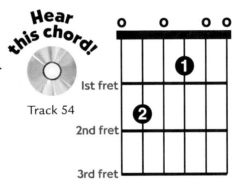

Hear this chord!
Track 54

Three Principal Chords in A

The three principal chords in the key of A are A, D, and E7. This next exercise uses the four-string D chord along with the five-string A and six-string E7 chords you just learned. Get comfortable moving from chord to chord before going to the next page.

Track 55

Moderato

Learn both parts of this duet and play along with the recording, your teacher, a parent, or a friend. To play the rhythm so it sounds like the real blues, play the groups of two eighth notes with the first note a little longer, and the second a little shorter (listen to the recording of "The 12-Bar Blues in A" to hear how it sounds). This blues rhythm is called *swing eighths*. Whenever you see "swing eighths" written at the beginning of a song, play the eighth notes with this rhythm.

The 12-Bar Blues in A (duet) Track 56

Moderato

42

Introducing
The Pentatonic Scale

The duet you just played used a *pentatonic scale*. Pentatonic means "five notes"—*penta* is Greek for five, so think of a pentagon that has five sides. The five notes in this scale are A, B, C-sharp, E, and F-sharp.

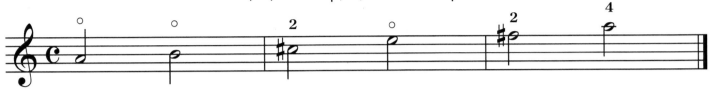

There are lots of different pentatonic scales, but this one sounds best over the three principal chords in A. You can play any of the notes in this scale along with these chords, which means you can *improvise* while the chords are being played. When you improvise, you are making up your own music!

Write down your own music in the blank staves below. Use the pentatonic scale you just learned. Then play your music along with the recording, your teacher, a parent, or friend. The accompaniment chords are written above the staves.

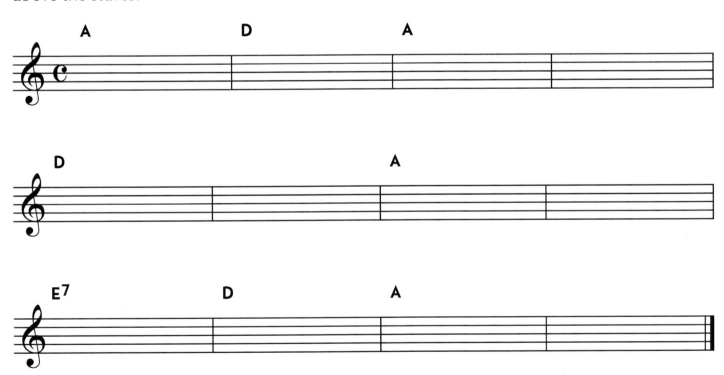

Now, go back and play with the progression again, but just improvise. Don't read the music you wrote down; just play the notes of the pentatonic scale any way you want. There are no rules—just have fun! Improvising is a great way to create your own new music a different way every time you play.

Over the Rainbow

🔘 Track 57

"Over the Rainbow" is one of the most popular songs ever written. It is in the key of G and uses the three principal chords of that key, and a few others too. Play the arrangement or the chords with a teacher or parent. Play the new A7 chord when you just play the accompaniment chords.

Words by E. Y. Harburg
Music by Harold Arlen

Moderato

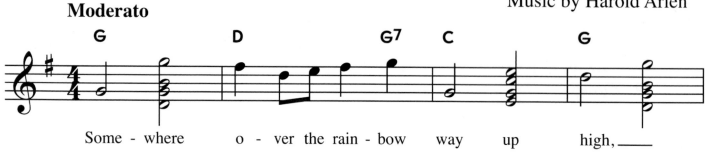

Some - where   o - ver the rain - bow   way   up   high, ___

There's   a   land   that I heard   of   once   in a lul - la - by. ___

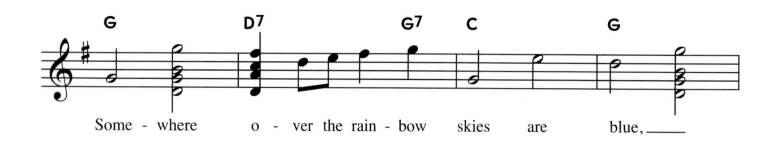

Some - where   o - ver the rain - bow   skies   are   blue, ___

and the dreams that you dare to dream real-ly do come true. Some-

day I'll wish up-on a star and wake up where the clouds are far be - hind me.___

___ Where trou-bles melt like lem-on drops, a - way a-bove the chim-ney tops that's

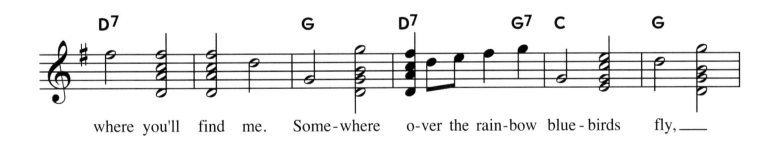

where you'll find me. Some-where o-ver the rain-bow blue - birds fly, ___

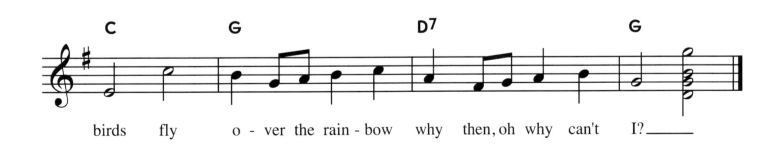

birds fly o - ver the rain - bow why then, oh why can't I?_____

Music Matching Games

Chords

Symbols

1. ♮   Dotted half note
2. 𝄢   Flat
3. ♪   Eighth Rest
4. 𝅗𝅥.   Crescendo
5. ♭   Natural
6. (staff with #)   Key Signature: F Major
7. 𝄾   Sharp
8. (hairpin)   Eighth
9. (staff with notes)   Loud
10. ♯   Key Signature: G Major
11. Allegro   Octave
12. (staff)   Dimenuendo
13. ♩.   Dotted Quarter Note
14. (hairpin)   Pentatonic Scale
15. 𝑓   Fast

Notes

Answer Key

Chords
1: page 41; 2: page 27; 3: page 41; 4: page 3;
5: page 18; 6: page 3

Symbols
1: page 22; 2: page 34; 3: page 7; 4: page 3;
5: page 22; 6: page 32; 7: page 37;
8: page 33; 9: page 43; 10: page 22;
11: page 3; 12: page 29; 13: page 12;
14: page 33; 15: page 3

Notes
1: page 3; 2: page 4; 3: page 17; 4: page 18;
5: page 22; 6: page 22; 7: page 22;
8: page 22; 9: page 22; 10: page 3

Guitar Fingerboard Chart

STRINGS

6th	5th	4th	3rd	2nd	1st
E	A	D	G	B	E

F	A#/B♭	D#/E♭	G#/A♭	C	F
F#/G♭	B	E	A	C#/D♭	F#/G♭
G	C	F	A#/B♭	D	G
G#/A♭	C#/D♭	F#/G♭	B	D#/E♭	G#/A♭
					A

FRETS

← Open →
← 1st Fret →
← 2nd Fret →
← 3rd Fret →
← 4th Fret →
← 5th Fret →

STRINGS

Fret	6th	5th	4th	3rd	2nd	1st
Open	E	A	D	G	B	E
1st Fret	F	A#/B♭	D#/E♭	G#/A♭	C	F
2nd Fret	F#/G♭	B	E	A	C#/D♭	F#/G♭
3rd Fret	G	C	F	A/B	D	G
4th Fret	G#/A♭	C#/D♭	F#/G♭	B	D#/E♭	G#/A♭
5th Fret						A

Chord Encyclopedia

Here are all the chords you know.

The three-string C chord

The three-string G chord

The three-string G7 chord

The three-string D7 chord

The four-string D chord

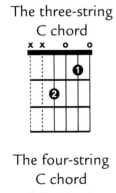
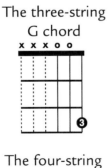
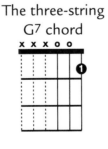
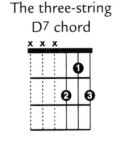
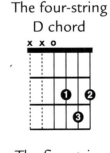

The six-string E7 chord

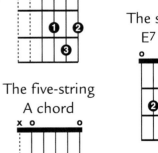

The four-string C chord

The four-string G chord

The four-string G7 chord

The four-string D7 chord

The five-string A chord

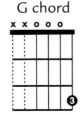
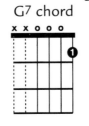

Certificate of Completion

This certifies that

_____

has mastered and perfected
Book 3 of Alfred's Kid's Guitar Course
and is hereby promoted into
Alfred's Basic Guitar Method Book 2

_____
Teacher / Parent

_____
Date